Jelly and Bean

Activities for A Series books 11- and B Series books 11-16

These **46** activities are to accompany the Jelly and Bean books 11 to 16 in the **A Extra Series** and books 11 to 16 in the **B Extra Series**. They cover the early to middle level of the work for Phonic Phase 3 of Letters and Sounds.

There are at least 3 activities for each of the books in these series. They mainly concentrate on the comprehension of the sentences and words in the stories.

Phonic work is included in the activities. Pupils are asked to write the correct vowels and consonants in some simple words.

New phonic content includes reinforcing the consonant combinations 'ng', 'ck' and 'qu'. Pupils are introduced to these consonants in writing and matching exercises.

The emphasis in these series of books is on the high-frequency words *'to, go, into, we, said, are, you'*, as well as the specific words *'down, out, for'*, which contain the vowel digraphs *'ow, ou, or'*.

The high-frequency words *'I, the, no, me, my'*, already introduced in books 5-10 of the **A Series** and the **B Series**, are also used for practice and reinforcement.

Marlene Greenwood 2014 ©

ISBN 978184305 282 1

Contents

11A
Activity 1 Write phrases with 'on' and 'off'.
Activity 2 Write missing words 'in, off, to'.
Activity 3 Write missing words 'went, to, see'.
Activity 4 Write 'went, to, and' in the passage.

11B
Activity 1 Match phrases to pictures.
Activity 2 Write missing words 'of, sits, hops'.
Activity 3 Write missing letters 'p, s, g, f, t'.
Activity 4 Match sentences to pictures.

12A
Activity 1 Write missing words 'hat, fun, see'.
Activity 2 Write missing words 'fun, see, big'
Activity 3 Find words, make a sentence.
Activity 4 Write missing words 'is, in, it'.

12B
Activity 1 Write 'e' in words.
Activity 2 Match sentences to pictures.
Activity 3 Write missing words 'is, It, am'.
Activity 4 Write missing words 'sits, egg, duck'.

13A
Activity 1 Write missing words 'of, not, bottom'.
Activity 2 Find and write 12 two-letter words.
Activity 3 Write missing words 'of, is, out'.
Activity 4 Write missing words 'top, bottom, duck cat'.

13B
Activity 1 Write missing words 'into, cannot'
Activity 2 Write missing words 'legs, pull, out'.
Activity 3 Write missing vowel 'a, e, i, o, u'.

14A
Activity 1 Write the missing words 'go, down, play'.
Activity 2 Write the missing words 'into, look'.
Activity 3 Match 'up' and 'down'.
Activity 4 Write missing words 'go, down, into'.

14B
Activity 1 Write missing words 'to, looks, go'.
Activity 2 Write missing words 'top, of, cannot'.
Activity 3 Write missing words 'man, van, go'.
Activity 4 Write missing vowel 'a, e, i, o, u'.

15A
Activity 1 Write missing words 'You, said, go'.
Activity 2 Write missing words 'you, Yes, said'.
Activity 3 Write missing words 'are, said, my'.
Activity 4 Write missing words 'said, me, my'.

15B
Activity 1 Write missing words 'cluck, quack, peck.
Activity 2 Write missing words 'clock, my, tick-tock'.
Activity 3 Write missing words 'off, not, stop'.
Activity 4 Write missing words 'see, rings, clock'.

16A
Activity 1 Write missing words 'little, for, quack'.
Activity 3 Write missing words 'look, you, quack'.
Activity 2 Write missing words 'lost, see, look for'.
Activity 4 Write missing words 'ducks, plays, ball'.

16B
Activity 1 Write missing words 'ding-dong, clang'.
Activity 2 Find and write 12 'ng' words.
Activity 3 Write 18 high-frequency words.

Name.............................. Date..............................

Write the correct words under each picture.

| on the log |
| off the log |

....

| off the pot |
| on the pot |

....

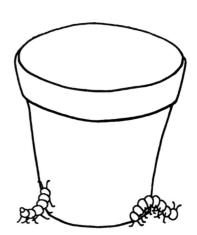

....

Name.............................Date............................

Use the words in the boxes to fill in the gaps in the sentences.

| off | | in | | to |

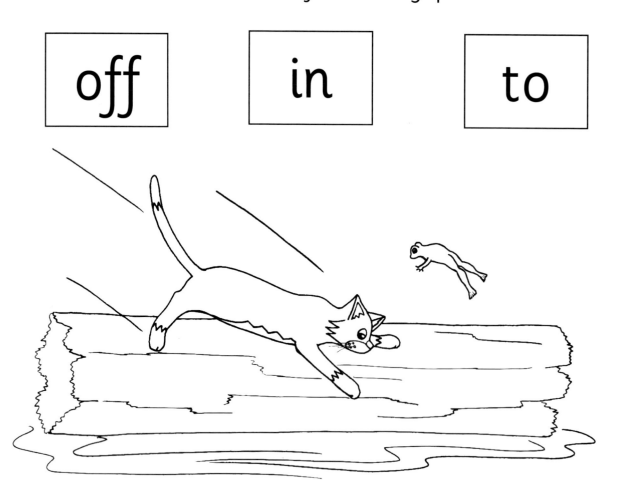

Jelly went ………. play on the log.

A frog went hop, hop, hop.

Jelly fell ………… the log.

Jelly fell ……… the mud.

Name.................................Date..............................

Write the correct word in each sentence.

| went | to | see |

The hen went .... see the cat.

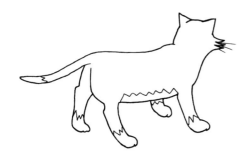 

The cat .... to see the rats.

The cats went to .... the hens.

11A activity 3 — Photocopiable activities from Jelly and Bean

Name.............................Date.............................

Write the correct word in each space.

| went | to | off |

Lotty went .... play on the log.

A frog .... hop, hop, hop.

Lotty fell .... the log.

Lotty fell in the mud.

Name.................................Date..............................

Draw a line from each phrase to the correct picture

| socks in the mud | a fat cat |

| a bag of pegs | ten pegs |

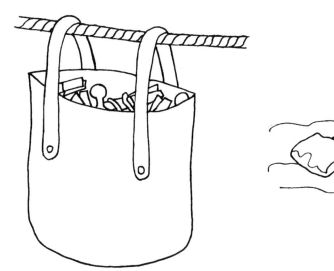

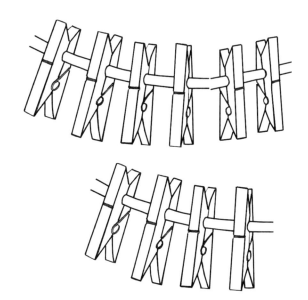

Name.............................Date.............................

Write the correct word in each sentence.

| of | sits | hops |

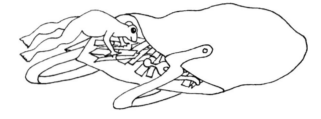

A frog hops in the bag .... pegs.

A fat cat .... on the bag.

The frog .... on the fat cat.

Name........................... Date............................

Write the missing letter in each word.

| p | s | g | f | t |

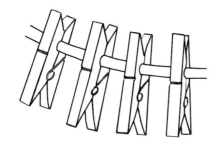

.......egs

.......at ca.......

ba.......

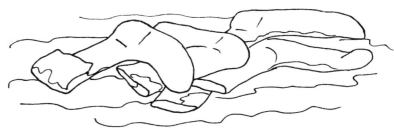

.......ocks

11B activity 3   Photocopiable activities from Jelly and Bean

Name.............................Date...............................

Draw a line from each picture to the correct sentence.

Colour the pictures.

A frog hops into the bag of pegs.

A fat cat sits on the bag.

The frog hops on the fat cat.

Name.............................Date.............................
Use the words in the boxes to fill in the gaps in the sentences.

| hat | fun | see |

Jelly can .... a big hat on the mat. Jelly jumps on the .... Jelly gets in the hat. Jelly has .... in the hat.

Name..Date...........................

Use the words in the boxes to fill in the gaps in the sentences.

| fun | see | big |

Bean can .... the big hat on the mat. Bean gets in the hat. Jelly and Bean have .... Oh no! The .... hat rips.

12A activity 2

Name.. Date..

Can you find the words in the picture? Write the words in a sentence on the dotted lines.

red   bag   a   in   play   Jelly   and   Bean

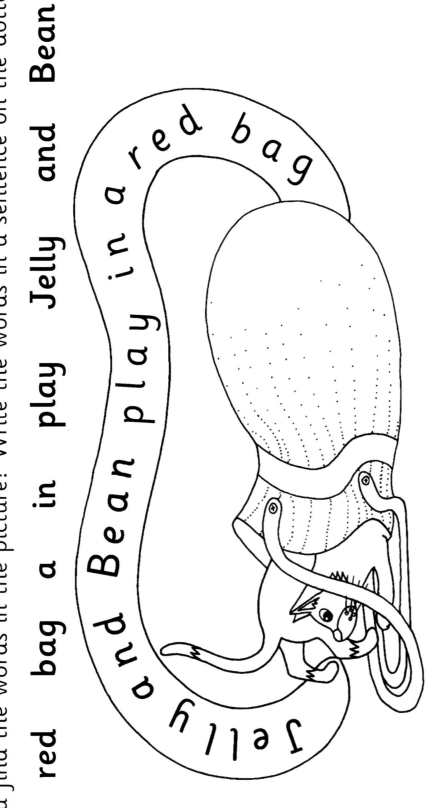

....

....

12A activity 3

Photocopiable activities from Jelly and Bean

Name.............................Date.............................

Write the correct word in each space.

| it | is | is | in |

Jelly jumps on the big hat.

Jelly has fun on ……… Bean gets in the hat. Bean has fun ……… it.

Oh no! The hat rips.

Jelly ……… sad. Bean ……… sad.

12A activity 4   Photocopiable activities from Jelly and Bean

Name.......................... Date..............................

Write **e** in each word. Colour the pictures.

...ggs

n...st

t...n

h...n

12B activity 1   Photocopiable activities from Jelly and Bean

Name..............................Date..............................

Draw a line from each picture to the correct sentence.

Colour the pictures.

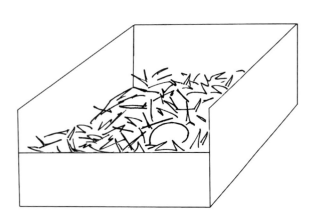

An egg is in the nest box.

A hen sits on the egg.

Oh! The hen has a little duck.

Name............................ Date................................

Write the correct word in each space.

| is | It | am |

This .... my bed.

I .... in my bed.

.... is soft.

I am asleep in my bed.

!2B sheet 3

Photocopiable activities from Jelly and Bean

Name.............................Date..............................

Write the correct word in each sentence.

Draw a line from each picture to the correct sentence.

| sits | egg | duck |

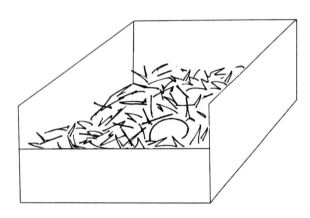

The hen has laid an .... in the nest.

The hen .... on the egg.

The hen has a little ....

Name............................Date..............................

Write the correct word in each sentence.

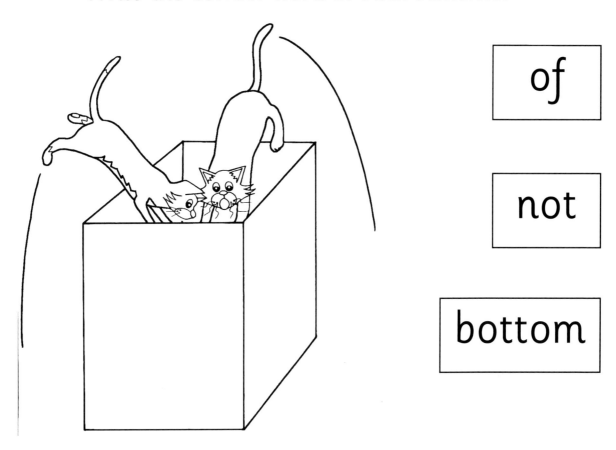

of

not

bottom

Jelly and Bean jump up to the top .... a big box. Oh no! The big box has .... got a top. Jelly and Bean are at the .... of the big box.

13A activity 1

Name.. Date..................

Can you find the words on the ladders?

in is it am me my
no up of at to on

Write the words at the bottom of the page.

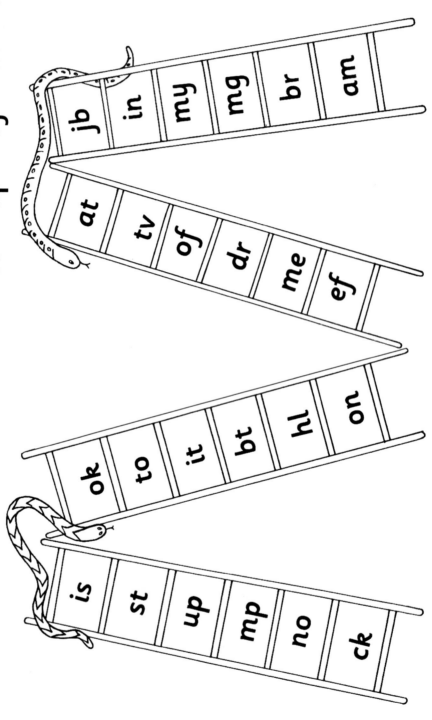

13A activity 2 — Photocopiable activities from Jelly and Bean

Name.......................... Date............................
Write the correct word in each sentence.

| of | is | out |

Wellington jumps up to the top .... the big box. Oh no! The box .... flat. Jelly and Bean get .... of the big box.

Name.............................. Date...............................

Use the words in the boxes to fill in the gaps in the sentences.

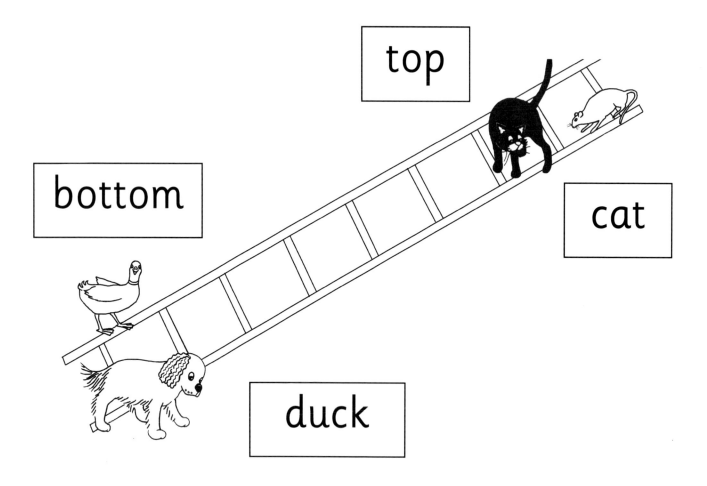

A rat is at the ....

A puppy is at the ....

A .... is at the top.

A .... is at the bottom.

Name.......................... Date..............................

Write the correct word in each sentence.

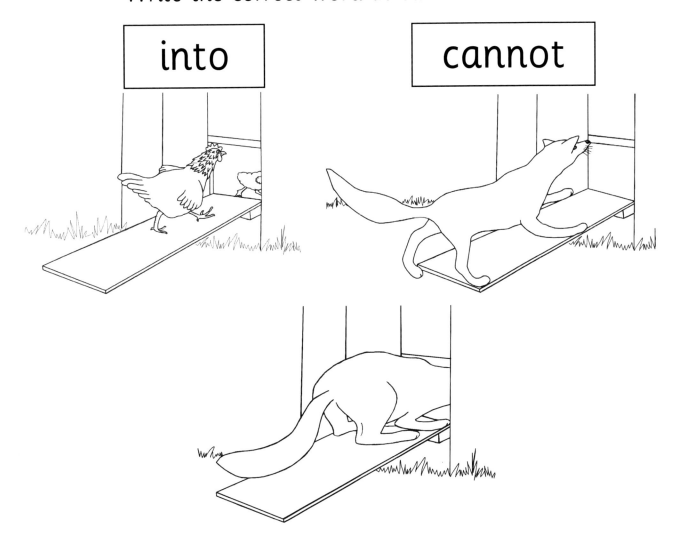

The hen and the little duck run .... the hut. The fox runs to the hut. The fox .... get in the hut.

Name.......................... Date..............................

Write the correct word in each space.

| legs | pull | out |

Jelly and Bean grab the fox's

.... Jelly and Bean

.... the fox's legs. The cats

pull the fox .... of the hut.

Name.......................... Date..............................

Write the correct letter in each word. .

| a e i o u |

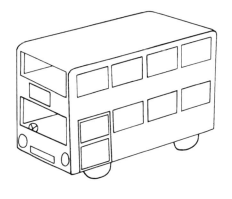

b...s

s...ck

f...x

h...ss

m...ss

13B activity 3 Photocopiable activities from Jelly and Bean

Name.............................. Date................................

Use the words in the boxes to fill in the gaps in the sentences.

| go | play | down |

Jelly and Bean .... up the hill.

Jelly and Bean .... at the top of the hill. Jelly and Bean go .... the hill. Bump, bump.

14A activity 1 Photocopiable activities from Jelly and Bean

Name.............................. Date................................

Use the words in the boxes to fill in the gaps in the sentences.

look

into

sleep

Kevin and Wellington .... in the kennel. The dogs go .... the kennel. The dogs .... in the kennel.

Name.............................Date.............................

Write the correct word under each picture.

| up | down |

....
....

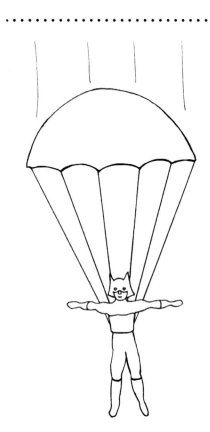
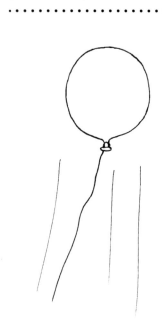

....
....

14A sheet 3
Photocopiable activities from Jelly and Bean

Name.........................Date...........................

Write the correct word in each sentence.

Jelly and Lotty .... up the hill.

Jelly and Lotty get wet. The cat and the dog go .... the hill.

Jelly and Lotty go .... the hut.

Name.............................. Date..............................

Write the correct word in each sentence.

Draw a line from each picture to the correct sentence.

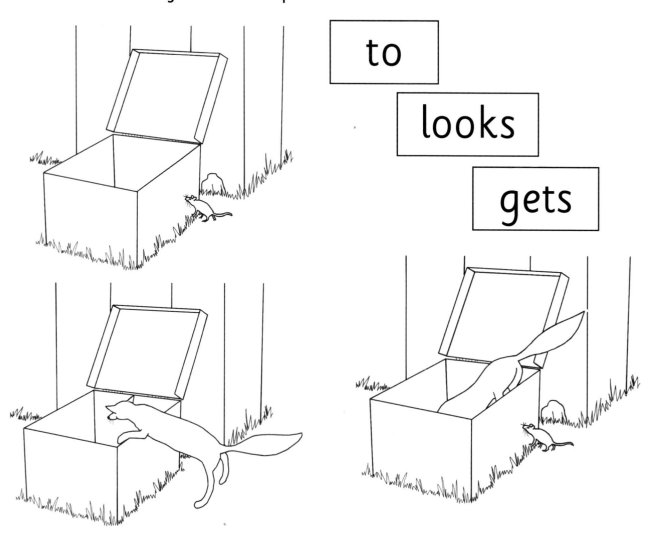

A box is next .... the hut.

The fox .... in the box.

The fox .... in the box.

14B activity 1   Photocopiable activities from Jelly and Bean

Name.............................. Date...............................

Write the correct word in each sentence.

| top |
| of |
| cannot |

Bean gets on the .... of the box. Jelly gets on the top .... the box. The cats sit on the top of the box. The fox .... get out.

Name.............................. Date..............................

Write the correct word in each sentence.

man

van

go

A .... puts the box in a van. The man gets in the .... Jelly and Bean see the man and the van .... away.

Name.......................... Date..........................

Write the correct letter in each word. .

| a e i o u |

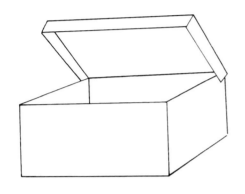

b...x

v..n

t...n

h...n

h...t

14B activity 4 Photocopiable activities from Jelly and Bean

Name.............................. Date..............................

Write the correct word in each sentence.

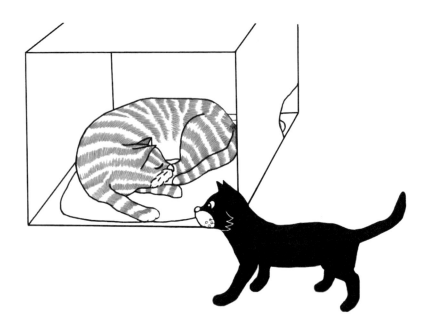

You

said

go

A big cat is in Bean's box.

Bean is cross. '............... are in

my box,' .... Bean.

'Go away, ... away.'

The big cat is sad.

Name.............................. Date................................

Write the correct word in each sentence.

you

Yes

said

'Can .... see me,' said the duck to the rat.

'.............., I can see you,' .... the rat. 'Can you see me?'

Name.......................... Date................................
Use the words in the boxes to fill in the gaps in the sentences.

| are | said | my |

'You .... on my nest,'

.... the hen to the duck.

'You are sitting on .... eggs.'

'Go away, go away' .

Name.............................Date.................................

Write the correct word in each sentence.

| said | me | my |

The big cat went to his bin.

'This is my bin,' .... the big cat. 'I can sit in .... bin. Nobody is cross with ....'

15A activity 4   Photocopiable activities from Jelly and Bean

Name.......................... Date..........................

Write the correct word in each sentence.

| cluck | quack | peck |

The hens said, 'cluck, ...'

The ducks said, 'quack, ...'

The hens peck, ..., peck.

15B activity 1   Photocopiable activities from Jelly and Bean

Name.......................... Date................................

Use the words in the boxes to fill in the gaps in the sentences.

| clock | my | tick-tock |

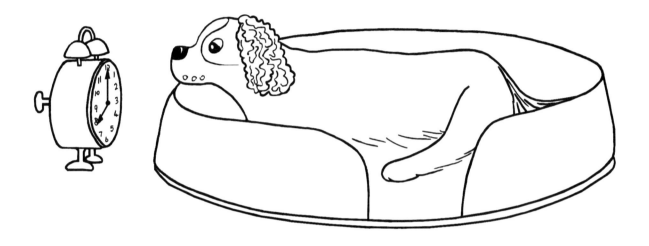

I have a .... next to my bed. I listen to .... clock.

'Tick-tock, ...'

I sleep on my bed. 'Zzz zzz.'

Name.............................. Date................................
Use the words in the boxes to fill in the gaps in the sentences.

My clock rings and I get .... my bed. My clock will .... stop ringing. 'Stop ringing clock. Stop, ... ,' said Lotty.

Name.............................. Date................................

Use the words in the boxes to fill in the gaps in the sentences.

I can .... my clock.

My clock .... It will not stop. I sit on my .... No tick-tock!

Name.......................... Date..........................

Write the correct word in each sentence.

| little | for | quack |

The .... duck has lost his mum . 'Quack, ...,' said the duck. The little duck is looking .... his mum. 'Quack, quack.'

16A activity 1   Photocopiable activities from Jelly and Bean

Name.............................. Date..............................

Write the correct word in each sentence.

| look | you | quack |

'We will help you to .... for your mum,' said Jelly and Bean. 'Thank ....,' said the little duck. 'Quack, ...'

Name.........................Date................................

Write the correct word in each sentence.

| lost | look | see |

Kevin has .... his big red ball. The ducks go to .... for the big red ball. The ducks cannot .... Kevin's big red ball. Kevin is sad.

16A activity 3   Photocopiable activities from Jelly and Bean

Name.............................Date.............................

Write the correct words in each sentence.

plays

ducks

ball

The .... have found the big red ball in the pond. Kevin .... with the ducks and the big red .... in the pond.

Name.............................. Date................................
Use the words in the boxes to fill in the gaps in the sentences.

| ding-dong |
| bong | clang |

Jelly rings the bells ding-dong,

'............................ .'

Jelly and Bean bang the gong.

'Bong, ...'

Wellington bangs the pans.

'Clang, ...'

16B activity 1   Photocopiable activities from Jelly and Bean

Name.............................. Date..............................

Say each of the words in the picture to a friend.
Write each word on a line at the bottom of the page.

long

ping

gang

king

gong

sting

bang

wing

song

ring

sing

clang

long ping bang wing gang song king ring gong sting clang sing

....

....

....

....

16B activity 2

Photocopiable activities from Jelly and Bean

Name.............................. Date..............................

Write each of these words on a dotted line.

Say each word to a friend.

go	I	no	the	to
see	we	me	my	
look		out		
said			down	
are		away		
for	you	into		

....

....

....

....

....